Chondhu Meets Koda

Smitha Kuttayya Boppanda

Illustrated by

Tamara Jose

notionpress
.com

INDIA · SINGAPORE · MALAYSIA

*This book is dedicated
to the land of my birth,
the childhood it afforded me
and all who were part of it.*

ACKNOWLEDGEMENTS

Embarking on writing a book was always a hazy dream in the corner of my mind. The list of people I have to thank for helping me get here is long.

To keep it brief, I am grateful to my mother, who has authored many books, and my father for always indulging me and for piquing a variety of interests in me while I was growing up. My father-in-law has always had a word of encouragement for me in every venture of mine. My husband is my rock and my pillar of strength, always admiring and encouraging me, and to him I am eternally grateful. My daughter is my lifeline, my teacher and the calm in my chosen chaos. I could not function if not for her support. My family, including my grandparents, my sister, aunts, uncles, cousins and extended family, have always had a good word for me – and that has helped me become the person I am. My friends are my bedrock and support system, and I am blessed to have all of them in my life.

Sumitha Menon, my editor, has supported me through all that I have done in the past twenty-two years. A multifaceted, extremely talented and dedicated person, Sumitha is the person I instinctively approached when I decided to publish my book. I have always trusted and relied on her editing skills in every little thing I have ever written, and it is no wonder that she was the one I chose to edit my book. I am ever so grateful to her. I also extend my utmost appreciation to Bibi Christa Xavier for a close reading of the book and for her extremely valuable inputs. This readable and free-flowing book is all thanks to both of them.

Tamara Jose, my illustrator, is another talented and creative darling. I am so grateful that she agreed to bring this story alive with her beautiful illustrations.

Finally, but not in the least, I express my deep gratitude to God and the universe.

Smitha Kuttayya Boppanda

CONTENTS

SUMMERTIME

Chondhu was eight years old and lived with her parents in distant Belgaum. All year round, she waited for her summer vacations because that was when she got to be with her dear Avayya.

'Avayya' was what Chondhu called her grandmother. Avayya lived in Kodag, popularly known as Coorg. Chondhu loved spending time with Avayya, as she enjoyed exploring the huge compound that surrounded Avayya's house. She was sure she would end up having thrilling adventures in the bargain. Avayya always draped herself in a traditional Kodava saree with a long-sleeved blouse, and wore shoes with stockings so that it was easier for her to walk around her estate.

She had salt-and-pepper hair and tied it as a topknot bun. Chondhu loved everything about Avayya. Avayya was strict and liked Chondhu to follow rules. At the same time, she allowed Chondhu to go out and explore on her own – which was always so much fun!

So, now that it was April, Chondhu excitedly told her mother what she wanted to pack in her suitcase and started planning all the different ways she was going to enjoy her time with her Avayya.

'Amma, do you think I will have an adventure at Avayya's house this time?' she asked, skipping from room to room.

'Why not?' asked her mother. 'You always have a wonderful time there, don't you?' On hearing this, Chondhu's face lit up with a big grin and her naughty eyes sparkled with mischief.

A week later, Chondhu, along with her mother and father, arrived in Kodag. There was a flurry of activity during the first few days of their visit, when they met relatives and friends. Soon after, her parents had to return home, as they needed to go back to work. Chondhu happily waved goodbye to them.

Then she looked at Avayya and squealed eagerly, 'Ahhhh Avayya! Now it's just you, me and Ponni! This is going to be so much fun!'

Ponni, the house help, came in just then, asking Avayya where to store the twigs and dry branches that she had collected from around the estate.

'*Adh alli ikkad. Neen Chondhuna oŕ round kootiyad po*' (Let that be there. You take Chondhu for a round now), said Avayya.

'Why Avayya? I know my way around!' said Chondhu.

'I don't doubt that!' said Avayya. 'I just want her to take you around and show you the new things on the property – where you can and can't go and all that. Now scoot! Off you go!' said Avayya.

A NEW DAY

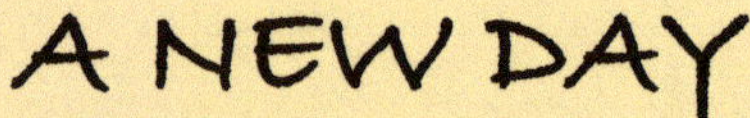

The next morning, Chondhu woke up to the aromas wafting into her room.

'I wonder what Avayya has made for me today,' she thought, as she got out of bed. She brushed her teeth, made her bed and went in search of Avayya.

Then she dashed back to her room again! Avayya would be sure to come in to see whether she had made her bed properly! And Chondhu also wanted to show Avayya that she had learnt to braid her hair!

Painstakingly, Chondhu straightened her bed from all sides, and then started brushing her hair. It had grown over the past year and she had refused to have it cut, promising her mother that she would look after it well. So now was her chance to prove that she could!

Chondhu went to the kitchen, looking for Avayya.

What was it that she smelt?

'Ahhhh, it was *kumbala* curry (pumpkin curry) and *otti* (rice flatbread)! What a lovely way to start my holiday!' thought Chondhu.

'Avayya! You made my favourite dish for breakfast!' she screamed and jumped on Avayya.

'Hey, hey! Calm down! So this is also your favourite dish now, is it?' she asked.

'Actually Avayya, everything you make becomes my favourite,' said Chondhu, as she grabbed three *otties* from the cane tray. 'Avayya, can I go exploring today?' she pleaded. 'I know you want me to finish my daily schoolwork and my music practice. So if I finish all that by ten o'clock, can I then go on my own?'

'Well, since you know the rules, you can finish your work and go. Be sure to be back in time for lunch,' said Avayya, smiling at her granddaughter. Finishing her breakfast quickly, Chondhu ran into Avayya's study room where a table and chair had been put out for her. She opened her books and did all the work assigned by her teachers for the holidays. Her mother had asked her to do some things too, which Chondhu finished in record time.

Now she had to attend her online *paat* class (music class).
Hoping that the internet would be slow that day, Chondhu
opened Avayya's laptop. Much to Chondhu's
disappointment, the internet was working perfectly fine.
So she had no choice but to sit down for class.

Chondhu finished her class, hardly able to concentrate,
for she was more excited to tell her music teacher her
plans for the day. Just as the class ended, Chondhu saw
that Avayya was at the door and had been listening to her
sing.

'You have progressed a lot since the last time you sang for me, *kunji*'
(little girl), said Avayya. 'Will you sing your new songs for me?' And then,
seeing Chondhu's crestfallen face, she quickly said, 'Not right now.
Whenever you have the time.'

Brightening up immediately, Chondhu said, 'Sure, Avayya! I will!'

Before another word could be exchanged, Chondhu changed into her
T-shirt and shorts, and darted out with her *thoore-kòl* (bamboo cane),* cap
and shoes.

'Juice!' called Avayya after her. 'I've made lemon juice for you.'

'Later, Avayya!' Chondhu called out, already halfway up the drive.

---

* In Kodag, every member of the family has their own *thoore-kòls*, which they
would have carefully chosen and picked up from the estate grounds.

THUD!

Racing up the steep driveway, Chondhu headed straight towards her favourite part of Avayya's estate. Avayya had stories to tell about every tree, such as who had planted them and how old they were. Chondhu could recall each of the stories. For now, however, it was the mango tree that caught her attention. Coming down the driveway, she had seen the tree laden with mangoes.

Chondhu wanted to climb the tree and get a few fruits for herself before Avayya called people from the village to pluck them. The pleasure of climbing a tree, searching for a ripe fruit, plucking it and eating it while perched on the tree was an unforgettable experience, and Chondhu wanted to relish every minute of it. She had planned it so well and had even worn an old T-shirt so that she would not have to worry about staining it. Looking up at the tree, she giggled loudly! Her T-shirt was yellow too, making it easier for her to be as messy as she wanted to be.

Yes! There was her tree! Oh yum! There were quite a few ripe mangoes hanging at a height low enough for her to grab! Not able to resist, she plucked off one that was nearest to the ground, 'Mmmmmmmm, this is so good!' Chondhu thought happily. Two mangoes later, she wanted to climb right up the tree and sit on 'her seat'. Chondhu's seat was at a point where three branches shot off from the trunk, making it a comfortable place to sit. Not stopping to take off her shoes, Chondhu started climbing higher and higher… Almost there!

Suddenly, she heard a loud sound – 'GRCHEEEEE!' Seconds later, Chondhu felt someone pushing her, and the poor unsuspecting girl fell crashing down to the ground below, screaming!

A VISIT TO THE DOCTOR

When Chondhu opened her eyes, she could not understand where she was. She turned on her side, 'OUCH! Aaahhhhhhh!' she cried out, and all at once she remembered what had happened to her! She saw the metal bar of the hospital bed and realised that she was at a doctor's clinic.

'Avayya! It was that stupid monkey, Avayya! It was so mean and nasty, and it scratched me and pushed me off the tree! It was not my fault!' Chondhu rambled.

'Calm down, *kunji*! Shhhhh,' said Avayya, hugging the little girl. 'I'm so glad you are up.'

'Avayya, we need to find that monkey and tie him up. I hate, hate, hate, hate him! My hand hurts so much and all because of him,' cried Chondhu, wailing afresh.

'No, no, *kunji*!' said Avayya. 'It was not Koda's fault. She is a new mother, and she was only protecting her baby. You can't be angry with Koda.' Seeing Chondhu's sad face, Avayya continued, 'No, no, I'm not saying it was your fault either. Koda has been around the property for a few weeks now. She is harmless and I'm sure she didn't mean to hurt you.'

Avayya gave Chondhu her medicine, and continued, 'She must have thought you were going to take her baby away and hence pushed you. Didn't Ponni tell you not to climb that mango tree?'

Chondhu's eyes went wide, as she realised her mistake, 'Oh yes, Avayya! Ponni had told me and I forgot! But I still hate, hate, hate Koda! She spoilt my holiday. Now my hand has to be in a plaster forever!'

'Oh, *kunji*! Luckily, you fell on a soft patch, and the injury is not very serious. Your plaster will be taken off in a week and then you can enjoy the rest of your vacation. You are a strong girl and Doctor says you will be up and about in no time!'

'That's great, Avayya! But I still hate Koda!' Chondhu persisted.

'Alright… let's go home now after seeing Doctor. We can look for Koda once we get back home.'

Doctor was a relative of Avayya. He examined Chondhu and spoke to her kindly. Once he was sure that Chondhu's injury was healing well, he spent some time exchanging pleasantries with Avayya. By this time, Chondhu, impatient to get home, was pacing up and down the room. Watching her fondly, both the adults cut short their conversation and bid each other goodbye.

'I know you will tell me to be careful, Uncle! I will. And I will be fine in no time at all! Thank you!' said Chondhu, already running down the steps.

Sitting in the front passenger seat of the car, Chondhu started struggling with the seat belt; so Avayya sat behind the wheel and helped her fasten it. During the drive, Chondhu was looking out of the window and exclaiming at every new thing she saw.

Suddenly, she looked at Avayya and said, 'Avayya, do you realise that you haven't taken me around town this time? Let's take the long way home, please? I want to see all the changes since I last came.' Avayya was tired, and wanted to get home quickly.

Just as she was about to refuse Chondhu's request, Avayya took one look at her granddaughter's earnest face and had no choice but to agree to take a drive around town.

THE SURPRISE

Two hours later, after driving all around their small town, Chondhu and Avayya reached the gate to Avayya's house. A huge roseapple tree stood on one side of the gate. Ponni came running to open the gate and to welcome Chondhu home.

Having had a lovely trip around town, Chondhu was in a great mood and rolled down the car window to greet Ponni.

'Hi Ponni!' she yelled, beaming from ear to ear. 'I'm going to be fine!' As she said this, she sensed a movement and looked up the tree.

Chondhu immediately alerted her grandmother, 'Avayya! She is there! Koda is there! Catch her, Avayya! Ponni! Bring that fat stick! Let's teach this Koda a lesson!'

Avayya and Ponni looked at each other. Chondhu looked from one to the other in disbelief.

Avayya spoke softly, *'Kunji…'*

Suddenly, they heard a soft thump, and it seemed almost as if the car shook for a moment. Chondhu was startled at what she saw. Who should she see but Koda, sitting comfortably on the bonnet of the car, with a baby monkey clutching onto her.

Chondhu started to scream when Koda put both her palms on the windscreen. Chondhu stared, mesmerised, as Koda made a gesture that seemed to say 'follow me' and then nimbly disappeared into the trees.

Before a stunned Chondhu could react, Avayya started the car and drove down the driveway. She got out of the car and opened the door for Chondhu. They were in the backyard. Chondhu quietly got out of the car as well, still trying to comprehend what had just happened.

Walking towards the back door of the house, she halted suddenly, 'Avayya!' she called out in a hushed tone, 'Avayya! Come here.'

Avayya walked up to see what Chondhu was pointing at. 'Mangoes … Koda … Look Avayya!' Chondhu exclaimed.

Slowly, Chondhu went closer to where the mangoes were neatly lined on the window ledge and looked up. Koda, holding onto her baby, was watching her keenly, almost as if she was looking for approval. Suddenly, Chondhu broke into a grin and said softly, 'Thank you, Koda! You are the best ever!'

Koda slowly came down, a step at a time, and offered the ripest, juiciest of the mangoes to Chondhu. Chondhu quietly took it and walked into the house, as Ponni opened the door.

Sitting at the dining table with the mango in her hand, Chondhu inspected it closely.

'Avayya, I think you were right! Koda didn't intentionally make me fall. It was just an accident. I think Koda is the best ever, and she is my new best friend.'
Even before she had finished speaking, Chondhu was racing out of the house.

 'Chondhu! Your hand! Be careful, *kunji*!' cried Avayya, trying to catch the little girl. Chondhu ran to where Koda was sitting, and plopped down beside her. They looked at each other for a long while before Koda carefully came down and gave Chondhu a hug.

'You know, Koda?' Chondhu gushed. 'You and I are going to be best friends and we are going to have a great time together! We can explore and have adventures together too.' Koda gazed at her as if she understood everything that was being said.

IN SEARCH OF NEW ADVENTURES

The next morning, Chondhu woke up suddenly. Her hand was not hurting quite so much! She remembered the happenings of the previous day and looked out of the window. Just as she had hoped, Koda, with her baby wrapped around her, was sitting right at her window waiting for her to wake up.

That very moment, Avayya came in with Ponni. 'Good morning, sweetie! How are you today?'

'Good morning, Avayya! Avayya, look! Koda is right here waiting for me!'

'Today, you can spend the day with Koda. Be sure to come back for your meals. Have a lovely time, my child. Ponni will make your bed, and I will brush your hair.'

An hour later, an impatient Chondhu was ready. Having had her breakfast, she asked Avayya if she could take some for Koda too. With a tiffin box full of *otties* and fruits for Koda, Chondhu ran out.

Koda was waiting for her, and they both set off happily in each other's company. Chondhu excitedly told Koda her plans, and Koda listened intently.

Looking at the two of them through the window, Avayya and Ponni chuckled.

'This is going to be an interesting holiday,' laughed Avayya.

ABOUT THE AUTHOR
Storyteller, educator, teacher trainer, mental health professional, dancer, baker, home chef and now, an author for the first time!

Smitha Kuttayya Boppanda dons many hats and revels in each of the roles she takes on. Her storytelling journey started in 2000 when she opened an after-school resource centre for children called Fun to Learn in Chennai, India. The joy she experienced out of narrating stories to a young audience encouraged her to take on storytelling assignments at other resource centres and at various schools in the city. Along the way, she started writing short stories for children, which she then narrated in her storytelling sessions. The next step in this journey was the launch of her YouTube channel, Smitha's Kaleidoscope, where she has uploaded her original stories along with those she enjoys telling. *Chondhu Meets Koda* is her first book for children. Smitha's books will be available as audiobooks too.

Smitha lives in Chennai, India. Her husband is a marketing professional, and her daughter is a furniture designer.

Smitha feels lucky to be able to convert so many of her hobbies and passions into vocations. It is rare for her to find herself at loose ends, as she enjoys gardening, sowing, binge-watching TV and reading too. She can be reached at skuttayya@gmail.com.

ABOUT THE ILLUSTRATOR
Tamara Jose is a part-time illustrator based in Mumbai, India. She has been associated with the field of Art from an early age, having also done her undergraduate degree in Creative Arts. Over the course of her professional life, she has created board games, website artwork and logos, predominantly for companies focusing on children and their needs. In the midst of a hectic work life, illustrating images for children serves as an escape into their magical world. *Chondhu Meets Koda* is her first children's book.